Ears

DOUGLAS MATHERS

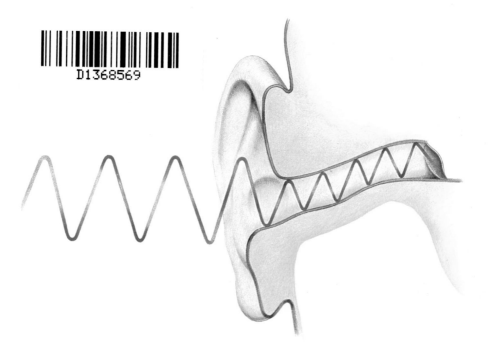

illustrated by
ANDREW FARMER and **ROBINA GREEN**

Troll Associates

Library of Congress Cataloging-in-Publication Data

Mathers, Douglas.
    Ears / by Douglas Mathers; illustrated by Andrew Farmer &
Robina Green.
        p.   cm.
    Summary: Explains how your ears function to hear sounds, maintain
balance, and measure distances.
    ISBN 0-8167-2092-4 (lib. bdg.)   ISBN 0-8167-2093-2 (pbk.)
    1. Ear—Juvenile literature.   2. Hearing—Juvenile literature.
[1. Ear.   2. Hearing.]   I. Farmer, Andrew, ill.   II. Green, Robina,
ill.   III. Title.
QP462.2.M37   1992
612.8'5—dc20   90-42176

Published by Troll Associates.

Edited by Neil Morris
Designed by COOPER-WILSON
Picture research by Jan Croot

Printed in the U.S.A.

10 9 8 7 6 5 4 3 2 1

Illustrators

Andrew Farmer front and back cover, pp 1, 2, 3, 5,
    12-13, 14, 14-15, 16-17, 17, 18, 18-19, 20-21, 22-23
Robina Green front cover, pp 4, 6, 6-7, 8, 9, 10, 11,
    13, 19, 20, 24, 26, 26-27, 28, 29
Additional illustrations by COOPER-WILSON

Picture credits:
Science Photo Library (Goran Bredberg) front cover,
    (Gordon Garradd) 7, (CNRI) 14, (Goran Bredberg)
    16
Siemens 29
ZEFA 21

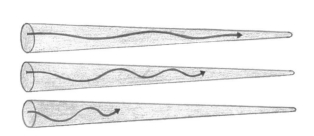

Contents

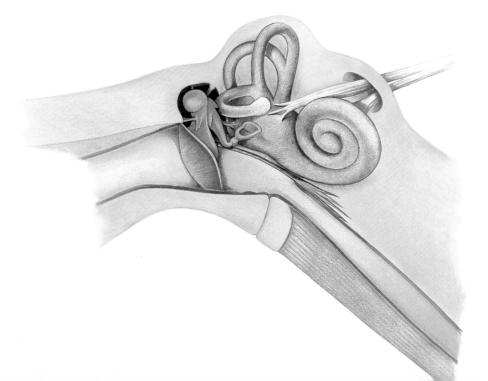

What are ears for?

Touch your ear. Did you know this is only part of a wonderfully complex organ that does other jobs for you besides hearing? The ear measures distance and is also your body's balancing organ. We would not be able to stand up without it, and it allows us to move around and know which way is up.

The external part of the ear (the part you can see and touch) is called the *outer ear.* It is shaped to collect sounds. These sounds are strengthened by the *middle ear.* The actual jobs of hearing and balancing are done by the *inner ear* deep inside your skull, behind and slightly below your eyeball.

Like your eyes, ears are special sense organs. Our senses are vital – every scrap of information about the world comes to us through them.

▼ This cutaway illustration shows that the inside parts of your ears are behind and slightly below your eyes.

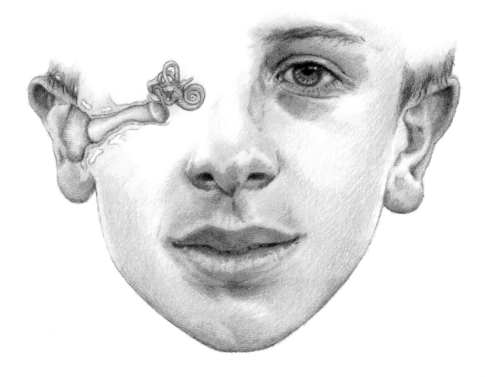

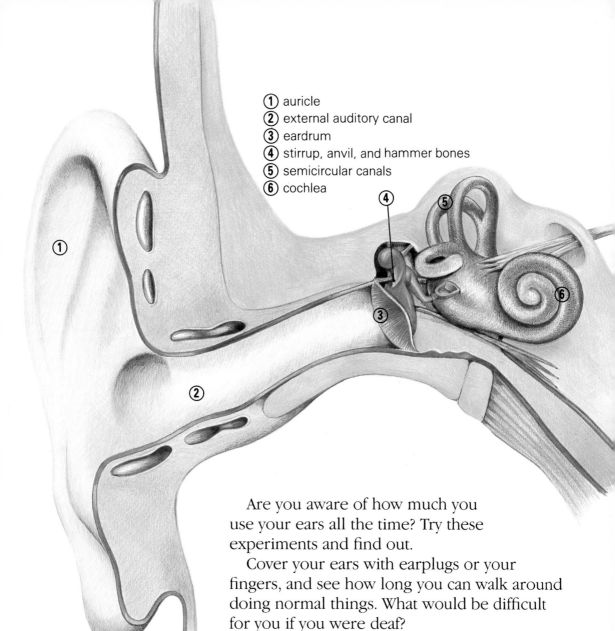

1 auricle
2 external auditory canal
3 eardrum
4 stirrup, anvil, and hammer bones
5 semicircular canals
6 cochlea

▲ The outer ear is made up of the auricle and auditory canal. The middle ear consists of the eardrum and ear bones. The inner ear contains the semicircular canals and cochlea.

Are you aware of how much you use your ears all the time? Try these experiments and find out.

Cover your ears with earplugs or your fingers, and see how long you can walk around doing normal things. What would be difficult for you if you were deaf?

Now blindfold yourself and let a friend lead you slowly around a familiar room. Tap objects as you go and note what you hear. Try to guess where you are in the room and what the objects are. Change places and discuss your experiences with your friend. Perhaps you can begin to understand how important the sense of hearing is.

Sound

The ear's most important function is to hear, and in everyday life we hear an enormous range of sounds. Think of the quietest and loudest sounds you know. What about the ones you like and dislike? Some sounds are so familiar that after a while you stop hearing them – for example, the refrigerator humming.

How are sounds made? Stretch a rubber band, then pluck it. You will see the band move up and down so fast that it becomes blurred. These *vibrations* make the sound you hear. All sound is made by objects vibrating. If you put your hand on your Adam's apple and say "aah," you will feel it vibrate.

Sound is carried to your ears by various means. The carrier can be a solid, liquid, or gas. The usual medium through which sound travels is air, which is a mixture of gases. The moon has no air, so the astronauts who went there had to communicate by radio.

▼ Air coming from your lungs makes your vocal cords vibrate. They are tensed and relaxed by special muscles, making the air hole bigger or smaller. A big hole makes a deep note, a small hole a high one – which is why a child's voice is higher than a grownup's. If these muscles are damaged by shouting, then the cords stay apart, making your voice low and husky.

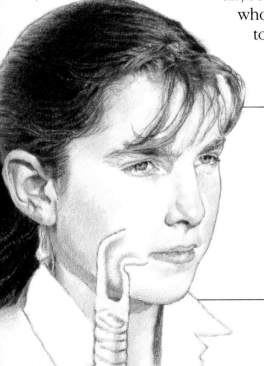

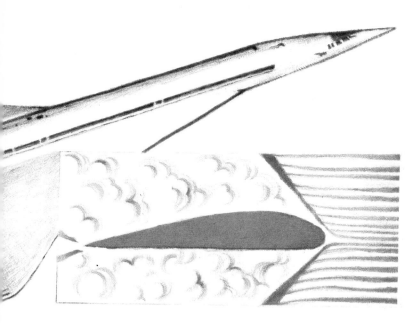

◄ As air moves over an aircraft's wing, it makes a noise, just as it does in your vocal cords. At the speed of sound, the wave traveling from the front of the wing bangs into the wave traveling from the rear of the wing. This makes a sonic boom.

► Clouds contain billions of water drops. Each drop has a small electric charge. When clouds move rapidly, these charged drops push into one another. The electric charge sparks to the ground, making a lightning flash and a bang. The flash travels to our eyes at 186,282 miles (299,792 kilometers) a second, the speed of light. Sound travels much more slowly.

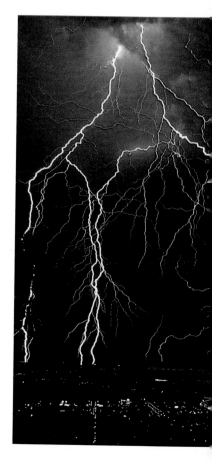

While electricity and light travel almost instantaneously, sound travels comparatively slowly. You usually hear thunder several seconds after seeing the lightning bolt that caused it. We see low-flying fighter planes before we hear them because they fly faster than sound.

Sound moves at about 760 miles (1,225 kilometers) an hour. When an airplane like the Concorde reaches this speed, the *sound wave* from the front of the wing hits the sound wave from the rear of the wing. This causes the *sonic boom* we hear as a plane flies through the *sound barrier.*

Sound waves

Sound travels in waves. We cannot see the waves in the air around us, but we can see them in water. Fill a glass with a liquid and hold the base of the glass with one hand. Wet a finger on your other hand, then run it around the rim. The noise is squeaky, but it becomes clear as the glass vibrates. When the sound is clear, look for a wave on the surface of the water. The wave is caused by the sound. Different amounts of water produce different notes. This is how a musical instrument called the glass harmonica works.

What makes the sound become a wave? The sound vibrations of a plucked rubber band cause the air particles around it to vibrate from side to side and back and forth. Each particle moves only a tiny distance and then back again,

▼ Different amounts of liquid in the glass produce different notes when you run your finger around the rim. The full glass produces a low frequency and a low note. The half-full glass produces a medium frequency. And the almost empty glass produces a high frequency and a high note.

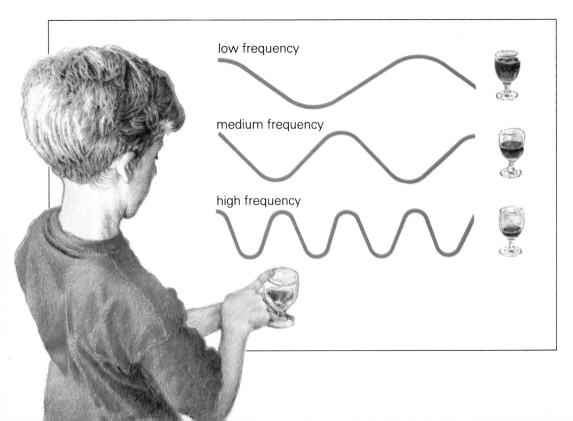

low frequency

medium frequency

high frequency

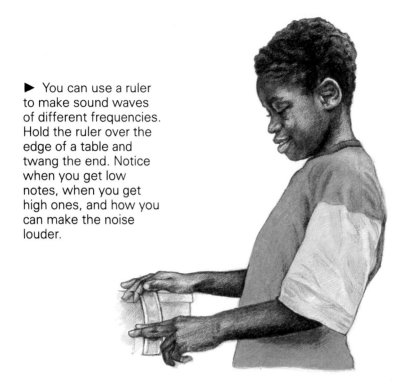

▶ You can use a ruler to make sound waves of different frequencies. Hold the ruler over the edge of a table and twang the end. Notice when you get low notes, when you get high ones, and how you can make the noise louder.

but it passes its energy to the next particle. The continuous up-and-down movements of the particles resemble waves. As the energy is passed from particle to particle, the sound gets weaker and weaker until it dies out. At this point the sound wave stops.

Waves have highs and lows. The height of a sound wave is the distance from a high to a low, and is called the *amplitude.* The greater the amplitude, the louder the sound. The distance between any point on one wave and the same point on the next wave is called the *wavelength.*

The number of waves reaching the same point in one second is called the *frequency.* Frequency is measured in units called *hertz.* Humans normally hear sounds with frequencies from 20 to 20,000 times per second, or 20 to 20,000 hertz.

▼ The height of a sound wave is its amplitude. In the experiment above, when a lot of ruler sticks out from the table, the end has a long way to waggle. So the number of waves per second is low and you get a low sound.

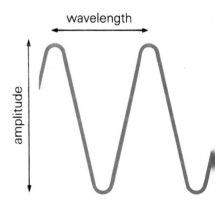

wavelength

amplitude

What can you hear?

High frequencies produce notes of a high *pitch,* while low frequencies produce a lower pitch. The rubber band we used to show sound vibrations can also help us to understand frequencies. Stretch the band very tightly and pluck it. The vibrations are too fast for the eye to follow. The high frequency of the waves produces a higher-pitched sound. What happens if you pluck a slack rubber band?

Some sounds are too high-pitched for the human ear. Humans can only detect these *ultrasounds* with scientific instruments. Certain dog whistles produce ultrasounds that a dog can hear, but the person blowing the whistle can't! Ultrasounds are also used in a ship's *sonar system.* By bouncing ultrasounds off objects and measuring the echo, the objects can be located and hazards avoided.

As our ears get older, they tend to hear less well. If you have a cold, you are not able to

► The blue area shows the range of sound frequencies that people can make, in hertz. The red area shows the range that people can hear. Both are compared with the ranges of certain animals.

▼ A low frequency produces a low-pitched sound.

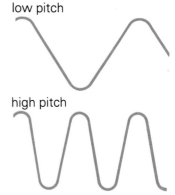

low pitch

high pitch

► Sound waves can pass through water and bounce off the sea bed. The time the sound takes to travel down and back can be measured and used to make a picture of the sea bed. The measuring instrument is called a sonic depth finder.

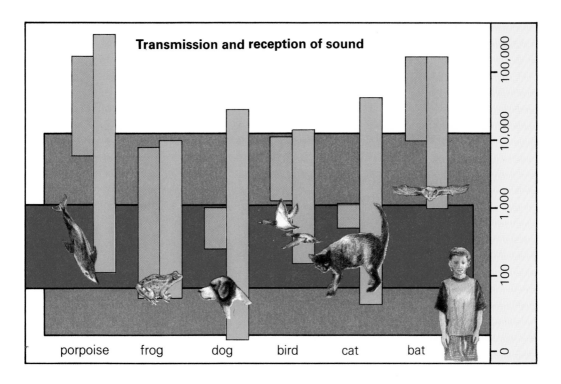

Transmission and reception of sound

porpoise	frog	dog	bird	cat	bat	

100,000
10,000
1,000
100
0

hear your usual range of frequencies. Also, people living in the country often have a better sense of hearing than people living in noisy cities. Because people have different levels of hearing, loudness cannot be measured scientifically.

However, we can measure the intensity of a sound by looking at its amplitude. The differences in amplitudes are measured in units called *bels.* This unit is named after the inventor of the telephone, Alexander Graham Bell. While speech is about 6 bels, pneumatic drills are roughly 12 bels. But this is not twice as loud. An increase of one bel means a sound is ten times louder than before. The pneumatic drill is more than a million times louder than speech. The bel is such a large unit that for everyday measuring we use a tenth of a bel, or *decibel.*

▼ We can compare the intensity of many sounds, measuring them in decibels. Very loud sounds can damage our ears.

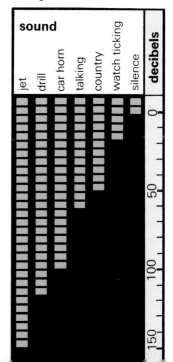

sound							decibels
jet	drill	car horn	talking	country	watch ticking	silence	

The outer ear

How does your ear hear sound? First of all, sound waves are gathered by the curly folds of the outer ear, or *auricle*. The auricle is made of skin and a rubbery material called *cartilage*.

Our ear-wiggling muscles are poorly developed, but many mammals can swivel their outer ears to collect sounds. If you know an animal well, stand behind it

and call its name to see how its ear muscles work. Some animals, like rabbits, need to hear their enemies approach, so they have ears designed to collect the most possible sound.

The auricle focuses the sound into a tube about half an inch (one centimeter) long inside your ear. It is called the *external auditory canal*. The canal is warm and wet. Germs love this kind of place, so ears protect themselves by producing wax. Sometimes too much wax builds up and stops sound. A doctor can loosen the wax and remove it by squeezing warm water gently into the ear.

▲ The auricle collects sound waves and sends them down the canal to the eardrum. We hear sounds from in front of us most clearly.

► The size of the outer ear does not determine how well an animal hears. Birds have small openings behind their eyes, but can hear quite well. Rabbits have good ear-wiggling muscles, so they can turn their ears without moving their heads.

It is dangerous to stick things into your ears to clean them. They may get stuck, injure the ear, or introduce germs.

The end of the external auditory canal is closed by a membrane, or fine sheet of skin, called the *eardrum*. This vibrates when the sound waves hit it.

► Fish do not have an outer or a middle ear. They have something like an inner ear, called a labyrinth. Some also have a lateral line system running along the sides of their bodies. They use this to sense vibrations and pressure changes in the water.

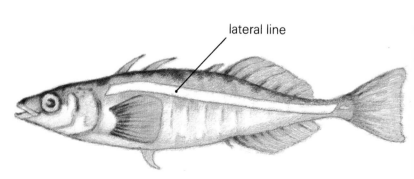

lateral line

The middle ear

On the other side of the eardrum is an air-filled cavity called the middle ear. It contains the three smallest bones in the body: the *stirrup,* the *anvil,* and the *hammer.* Can you see how they got their names? They link together to form a chain about a quarter of an inch (half a centimeter) long that is joined to the eardrum by the hammer bone.

The vibrating eardrum makes the delicate little bones move. This enlarges, or *amplifies,* eardrum movements up to twenty times and allows us to hear very quiet sounds. Tiny muscles stop the bones from moving too much, so loud sounds don't damage our ears.

When the air pressure outside changes, as when we're in an airplane or riding in an elevator, the air inside the middle ear expands or contracts to match. This could damage the tiny bones or even burst the eardrum, but a

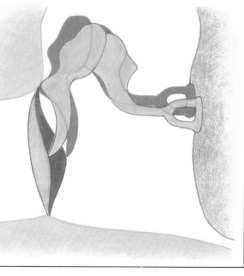

▼ A photograph (*left*) of the ear bones, and an illustration of how they pass on vibrations. The eardrum vibrates the hammer, that moves the anvil, that moves the stirrup, that vibrates the cochlea.

Middle-ear bones

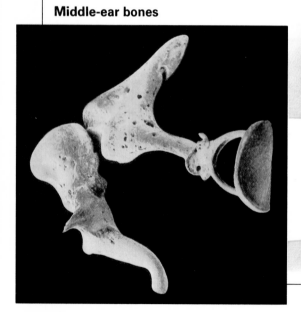

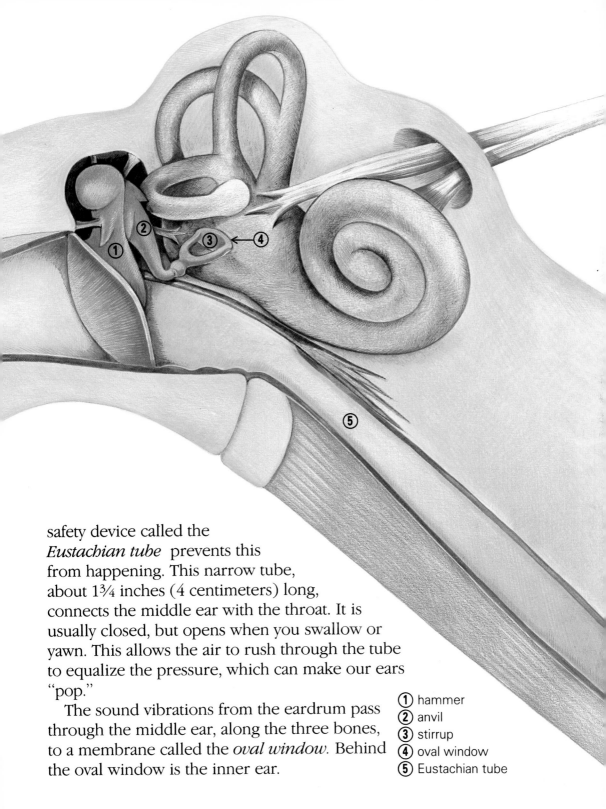

safety device called the
Eustachian tube prevents this
from happening. This narrow tube,
about 1¾ inches (4 centimeters) long,
connects the middle ear with the throat. It is
usually closed, but opens when you swallow or
yawn. This allows the air to rush through the tube
to equalize the pressure, which can make our ears
"pop."

The sound vibrations from the eardrum pass
through the middle ear, along the three bones,
to a membrane called the *oval window*. Behind
the oval window is the inner ear.

① hammer
② anvil
③ stirrup
④ oval window
⑤ Eustachian tube

15

The inner ear: the cochlea

The bony inner ear lies deep within your skull. Part of it is made of a spiral tube shaped like a snail shell. This is called the *cochlea,* from the Latin word for snail. Inside the cochlea there is a strip of skin covered with fine hairs, called the *organ of Corti* after the Italian doctor who first described it. The rest of the "snail" is filled with a fluid called *lymph*.

When the bones in the middle ear move, they stretch the skin on the oval window. This makes the lymph move, which in turn causes the hairs on the organ of Corti to move, like wind blowing through a field of wheat. At the bottom of each hair is a nerve cell which senses any movement. The cell then sends an

① stirrup
② oval window
③ organ of Corti
The cochlea is filled with lymph.

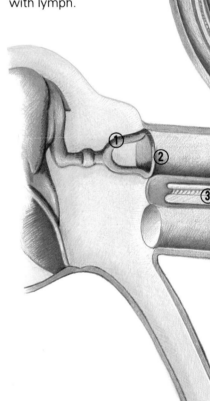

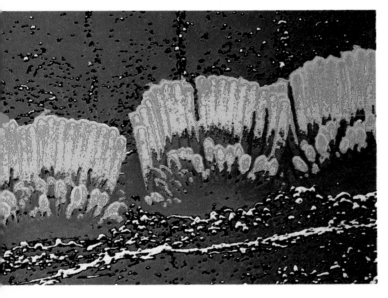

▲ A row of hair cells in the inner ear, seen through an electron microscope and magnified over 5,000 times. Each cell contains up to 100 hairs, with shorter hairs in front and larger ones behind.

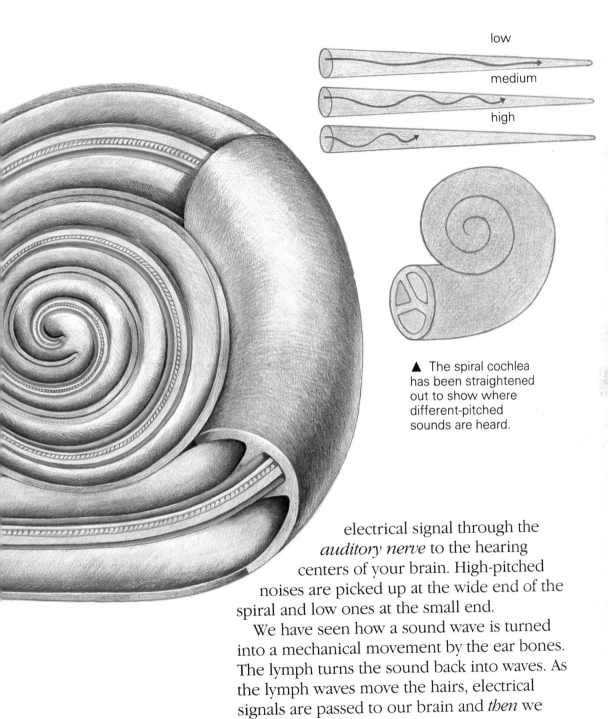

▲ The spiral cochlea has been straightened out to show where different-pitched sounds are heard.

electrical signal through the *auditory nerve* to the hearing centers of your brain. High-pitched noises are picked up at the wide end of the spiral and low ones at the small end.

We have seen how a sound wave is turned into a mechanical movement by the ear bones. The lymph turns the sound back into waves. As the lymph waves move the hairs, electrical signals are passed to our brain and *then* we hear!

The inner ear: the canals

Next to the cochlea are three *semicircular canals*. They help you keep your balance by letting the brain know what movements your body is making.

Like the cochlea, the canals have a bony part lined with fine hairy skin and filled with lymph. The curved tubes of the canals are at right angles to one another, so the slightest movement of your head will affect the lymph in at least one of them. The moving lymph bends sensory hairs. Nerves on these hairs inform the brain of the head's movements.

Gravity is the force that pulls us toward the center of the Earth, and your sense of balance tells you where you are in relation to that force. Tiny crystals of calcium carbonate, called *otoliths,* press on particular hairs at the base of the canals.

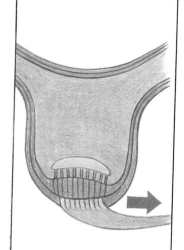

▲ This section through a semicircular canal shows an otolith pressing on hair cells at the base. Nerves from the hair cells send signals to the brain to tell it what position the head is in.

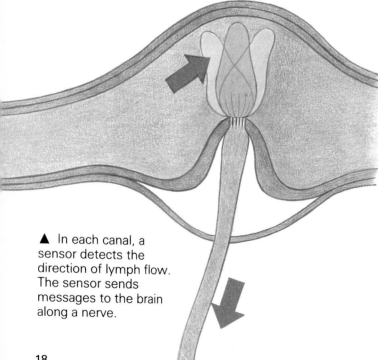

▲ In each canal, a sensor detects the direction of lymph flow. The sensor sends messages to the brain along a nerve.

▶ The three semicircular canals are at right angles to one another, like the three sides at the corner of a box. Because of this, the canals can measure movement in any direction.

When your head tilts, the crystals move under the influence of gravity and press on other hairs. The nerves from the hairs let the brain know what position the head is in.

Even with your eyes closed, or under water, your otoliths will help you know the position of your head. But when you drive fast over a steep hill, you sometimes get a very strange sensation. This is because the otoliths "float" for a moment, which confuses your sense of gravity.

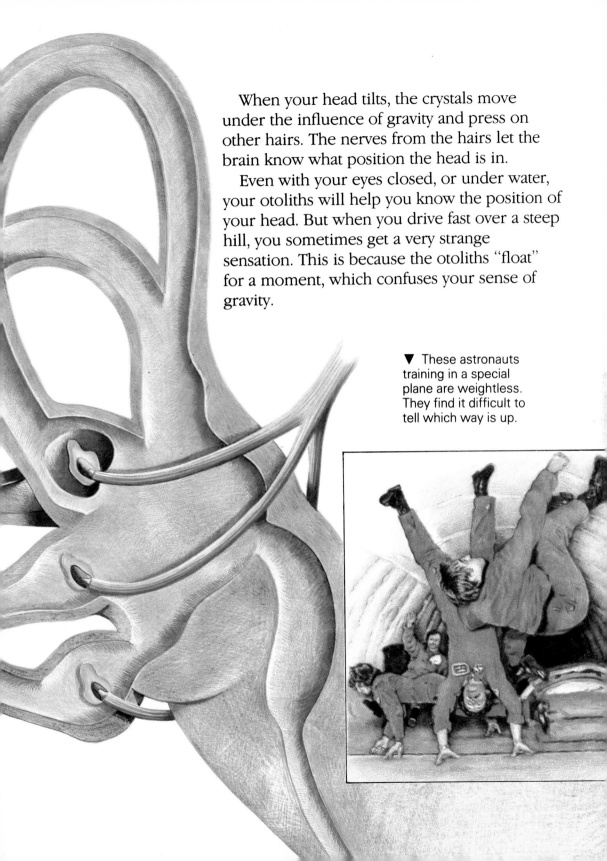

▼ These astronauts training in a special plane are weightless. They find it difficult to tell which way is up.

The brain and balance

The brain keeps us from falling over by adding all the information from the semicircular canals together with other sensory input from the rest of the body.

This is done in the *cerebellum,* a part of the brain at the back of your head. The cerebellum of a cat is especially large, and cats are famous for their excellent sense of balance.

When the signals coming from the semicircular canals don't agree with the signals coming from the rest of the body, we feel dizzy and sick. This is why we sometimes get carsick or seasick if there is rapidly changing motion around us. We may feel dizzy when the blood supply to our brain is too low, such as when we stand up too quickly. We also feel sick and dizzy if the ear is infected or the brain is affected by alcohol.

▼ Nerve signals from the ear reach the brain at the medulla (**1**). Balance is controlled in the cerebellum (**2**). The occipital lobe (**3**), at the back of the brain, is where we see. A special area (**4**) helps us to recognize sounds, to recognize written words (**5**), and to produce

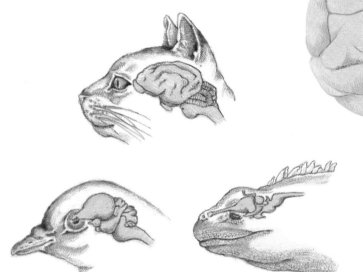

⑨

⑥

◄ Animals have different-sized brains and cerebellums. A cat's cerebellum is especially large.

speech (**6**). The motor cortex (**7**) and sensory cortex (**8**) help us to balance and turn our head toward sounds. The frontal lobe (**9**) is where we put sounds and pictures together, to understand what they all mean.

Find a safe place and spin around. Be careful! When you stop, the room seems to keep going around and around. You might even fall over if you have spun too fast!

The reason for this is that the lymph continues to move after you have stopped moving. The brain believes the messages from the moving lymph in the ear, rather than the messages of the eye, and tries to move the eyes to keep up.

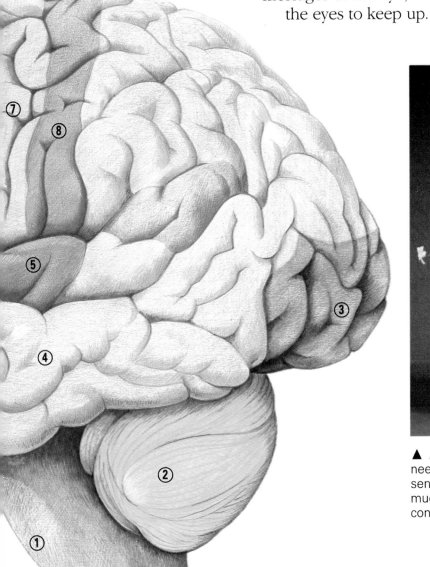

▲ A ballet dancer needs an excellent sense of balance as much as muscular control and technique.

The brain and sound

Signals from the cochlea travel along the auditory nerves from each ear to part of the brain called the *medulla,* at the top of the spinal cord. Run your finger up the back of your neck until it touches the bottom of your skull. The medulla is about half a finger-length beneath your finger. It is a junction for nerves from all over the body, and reroutes incoming signals to many parts of your brain.

The parts of the brain near the medulla are concerned with survival. We are not conscious of their working. This is why we jump in response to a loud sound before we recognize it, or turn our heads without thinking when someone calls our name. A sound we might ignore in daytime, such as a creaking floorboard, might scare us in the middle of the night.

An absence of an accustomed sound can be equally frightening. One night, the police in a small town received about 200 phone calls from one street reporting burglars in the house or other disturbances. Mystified, the police eventually discovered that a noisy train had passed the back of the houses at the same time every night for 20 years – until that night, when it had been canceled!

Listening to other people is a special skill that depends upon using the conscious part of our brains. For example, you may be talking to a friend when you hear your name mentioned by two other people nearby. You may well shift your attention to those speakers in case you hear something that would affect your well-being.

You could still appear to be listening to your friend, but even though you are hearing both speakers, you are listening to only one of them.

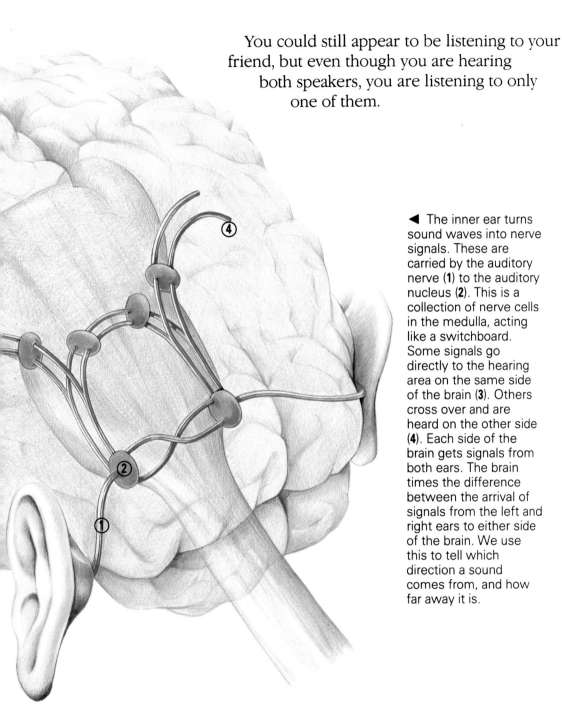

◀ The inner ear turns sound waves into nerve signals. These are carried by the auditory nerve (**1**) to the auditory nucleus (**2**). This is a collection of nerve cells in the medulla, acting like a switchboard. Some signals go directly to the hearing area on the same side of the brain (**3**). Others cross over and are heard on the other side (**4**). Each side of the brain gets signals from both ears. The brain times the difference between the arrival of signals from the left and right ears to either side of the brain. We use this to tell which direction a sound comes from, and how far away it is.

Sound patterns

The medulla transmits the signal from the ears to the *temporal lobes* of the brain, located just behind our ears. Here the brain tells us which sounds we heard, how loud they were, and in what order they arrived. This is like recognizing the letters in a word.

We think and remember in patterns. Just as letters are put together to make a word, so sounds are put together in patterns. This is done in the "sound association area" on the left-hand side of the brain, in front of your left ear.

Just as words are put together to make a story, so the front part of your brain, just above your eyes, puts the sound patterns together. This is where we understand what we have heard, and then choose what to do about it.

The great German composer, Ludwig van Beethoven (1770-1827), slowly went deaf. By the time he was 50, he was almost totally deaf and had to carry on all conversation in writing. But Beethoven could remember sound patterns so well that he could still write music. He composed some of his greatest works when he was already deaf.

From the moment you are born, your brain stores memories of all the sounds you hear. By the time you are an adult, you will be able to recognize about half a million different sounds. The working of the brain is still not fully understood, but at the moment it is thought that memory is stored throughout the brain.

How we feel about the patterns does alter how easy it is to remember them. You probably find it easier to remember the names of your favorite movie stars than the names of the politicians who run your country!

▼ Musicians use a special musical alphabet of notes and lines to tell others how to make sounds. The position of a note on the lines tells you which pitch to play, and the type of note tells you for how long to play it.

Old Macdonald's Farm

NOTE	C	C	C	G	A	A	G		E	E	D	D	C			C	C	C	G
COUNT	1	2	3	4	1	2	3	4	1	2	3	4	1	2	3	4	1	2	3	4

	A	A	G		E	E	D	D	C		D	C	C	C		C	C	C
	1	2	3	4	1	2	3	4	1	2	3	4	1	2	3	4	1	2	3	4

	C	C	C	C	C	C	C	C	C	C	G	A	A	G		E	E	D	D	C
	1	2	3	4	1	2	3	4	1	2	3	4	1	2	3	4	1	2	3	4

Distance

You use several of your senses to measure distance, including sight and smell. Did you know you use hearing as well?

The brain figures out the distance and direction of a sound by measuring the difference in time that the sound takes to reach each ear. For example, if a sound is closer to the right ear, that ear will hear the sound a fraction of a second sooner than the left ear.

Here is a simple experiment to show this. Stand facing a sound. A radio will do. Close your eyes. Do you still know where the radio is? Put a hand over one ear and a cardboard tube over the other. Which way does the radio seem to move? Now try it the other way around.

A sound is coming from behind. Each ear is the same distance from it, so signals from both ears reach both halves of the brain at the same time.

When we turn our head, this changes the distance from the sound source to one ear and helps us check where the sound is coming from.

The sound is coming from one side, and signals from the right ear are louder.

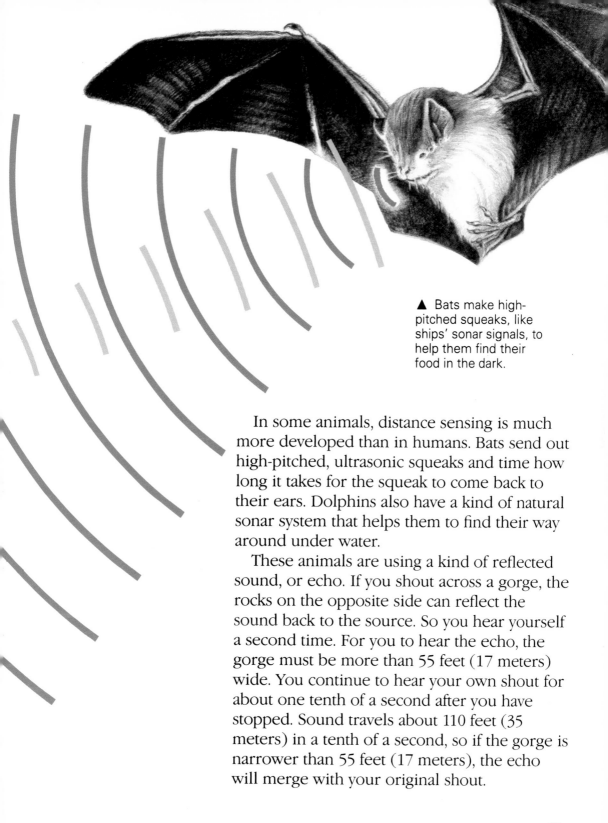

▲ Bats make high-pitched squeaks, like ships' sonar signals, to help them find their food in the dark.

In some animals, distance sensing is much more developed than in humans. Bats send out high-pitched, ultrasonic squeaks and time how long it takes for the squeak to come back to their ears. Dolphins also have a kind of natural sonar system that helps them to find their way around under water.

These animals are using a kind of reflected sound, or echo. If you shout across a gorge, the rocks on the opposite side can reflect the sound back to the source. So you hear yourself a second time. For you to hear the echo, the gorge must be more than 55 feet (17 meters) wide. You continue to hear your own shout for about one tenth of a second after you have stopped. Sound travels about 110 feet (35 meters) in a tenth of a second, so if the gorge is narrower than 55 feet (17 meters), the echo will merge with your original shout.

What can go wrong with ears?

Pain in the ears can be caused by blows to the outer ears, wax in the external auditory canal, and infections or changes of pressure in the middle ear.

If you have frequent colds, the middle ear can get infected. A fluid called pus collects, and it can be so thick that it cannot drain down the Eustachian tube. This can cause temporary deafness, but it disappears when the infection clears up.

The most common kind of deafness is *conductive,* which happens when sound can't get into the inner ear. It can be caused by wax blocking the ear, a torn eardrum, or if the three little bones in the middle ear are broken. Sometimes the bones can be rebuilt or replaced surgically.

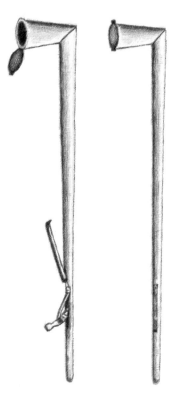

walking cane

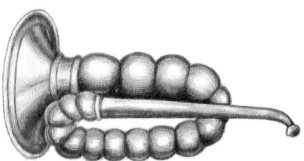

ear trumpet

▲ These ingenious machines are old-fashioned hearing aids — ear trumpet, a hearing horn, cane, and tube. They work by collecting lots of air, acting as a bigger outer ear, and making the sound louder.

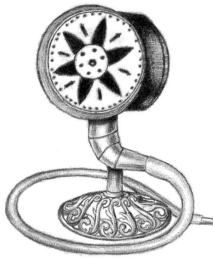

ear tube

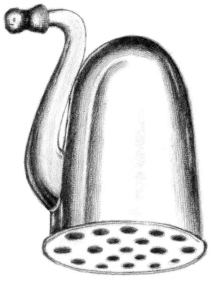

hearing horn

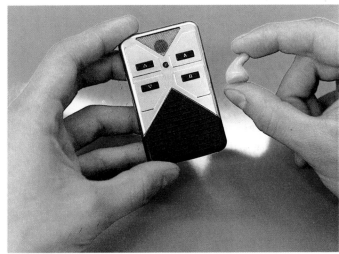

conversation tube

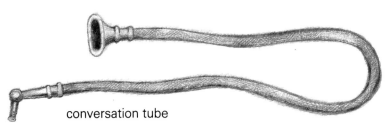

▲ This modern electronic hearing aid sits inside the outer ear. It has a microphone and loudspeaker in it, and a remote-control device for altering volume.

Sensory deafness can occur after years of loud noise, or with age. Often a hearing aid can help people with this kind of deafness.

About one in five hundred people is born deaf. Earlier in the book we did an experiment about deafness, but imagine what it would be like to be permanently deaf. Broken legs can be seen and get sympathy. But we can't see broken internal ears, so people often wrongly assume that deaf people are being rude or that they are stupid. Deaf people have had to find special ways to communicate, such as sign language and lip-reading.

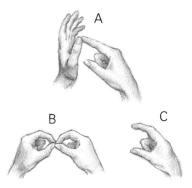

▲ This version of a sign language spells out letters of the alphabet. Others use single signs and gestures to mean whole words.

Glossary

amplify   to enlarge, to make (a sound) louder.

amplitude   the distance from the top to the bottom of a sound wave.

anvil (or incus)   one of three tiny bones in the middle ear.

auditory nerve   the nerve that carries messages from the ear to the brain.

auricle   the part of the ear that sticks out from your head.

bel   the unit for measuring the relative loudness of sounds.

cartilage   tough elastic tissue; this gives the auricle its shape.

cerebellum   a part of the brain at the back of our head that helps us balance.

cochlea   the spiral tube in the inner ear that is full of lymph and contains the organ of Corti.

conductive deafness   loss of hearing because of blockage or damage to the parts of the ear that carry sound waves from the auricle to the oval window.

decibel   one tenth of a bel.

eardrum   a fine sheet of skin, stretched like a drum across the inner end of the external auditory canal; sound waves make the eardrum vibrate.

Eustachian tube   a narrow tube joining the middle ear to the back of the throat.

external auditory canal   the tube in the outer ear leading to the eardrum.

frequency   the number of sound waves reaching the same point in one second, measured in hertz.

hammer (or malleus)   one of three tiny bones in the middle ear.

hertz   the unit of frequency; one hertz equals one wave per second.

inner ear   the part of the ear that consists of the cochlea and semicircular canals.

lymph   a clear fluid that fills the inner ear.

medulla   the part of the brain, at the top of the spinal cord, that receives signals from the auditory nerve and transmits them to the temporal lobes.

middle ear   the air-filled cavity between the eardrum and the inner ear, containing the ear bones.

organ of Corti   a hair-covered strip curled inside the cochlea, where sound signals are changed into nerve impulses.

otoliths   crystals of calcium carbonate (chalk) in the semicircular canals.

outer ear   the part of the ear you can see, made up of the auricle and the external auditory canal.

oval window   a fine sheet of skin stretched across a hole in the cochlea; the ear bones move this membrane.

pitch   sound frequency, used to describe differences in musical notes.

semicircular canals   three curved tubes in the inner ear that help us keep our balance.

sensory deafness   loss of hearing due to damage to hair cells or to the auditory nerve.

sonar system   a natural or man-made system that measures distances by timing echoes.

sonic boom   the noise made by an airplane breaking the sound barrier.

sound barrier   a difficulty airplanes meet when they fly as fast as sound waves. The plane has to push the sound wave it makes out of the way; this needs more power from the engines.

sound wave   a regular disturbance in the molecules of air or water made by a moving object.

stirrup (or stapes)   one of the three tiny bones in the middle ear.

temporal lobes   the parts of the brain just behind the ears, that recognize sounds and are involved in memory.

ultrasound   a sound whose pitch is too high for human ears to hear.

vibration   rapid movement back and forth.

wavelength   the distance between two identical points in a pattern of waves — from the top of one wave to the top of the next, or the bottom of one to the bottom of the next.

Index